Peter Serafinowicz is an English actor, comedian, writer and director.
He co-wrote the critically acclaimed TV show *Look Around You* with Robert Popper;
starred in *The Peter Serafinowicz Show*, which was nominated for a BAFTA and won
the Rose d'Or prize for Best Entertainer; directed the music video for Hot Chip's 'I Feel
Better'; appeared in *Spaced*, *Shaun of the Dead*, *Couples Retreat* and *Bad Sugar* – and
provided the voice for Darth Maul in the film *Star Wars Episode 1: The Phantom Menace*.
He lives in London.

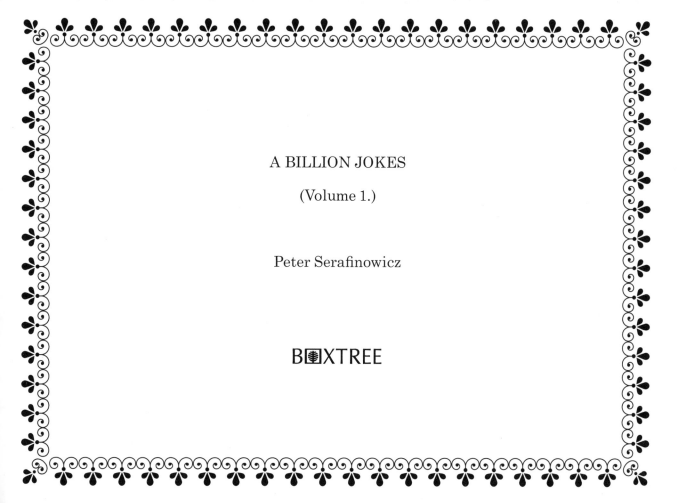

A BILLION JOKES

(Volume 1.)

Peter Serafinowicz

B⬛XTREE

First published 2012 by Boxtree,
an imprint of Pan Macmillan, a division of Macmillan Publishers Limited
Pan Macmillan, 20 New Wharf Road, London N1 9RR
Basingstoke and Oxford
Associated companies throughout the world

www.panmacmillan.com

ISBN 978-1-4472-2348-1

Design by Alex Morris

Printed and bound in Italy by Printer Trento

Visit **www.panmacmillan.com** to read more about all our books and to
buy them. You will also find features, author interviews and news of any
author events, and you can sign up for e-newsletters so that you're always
first to hear about our new releases.

To Sarah

A BILLION JOKES

(Volume 1.)

I'm still angry at my parents for not buying me expensive rollerblades.

Cheapskates.

How did I manage to glue my mouth shut?

My lips are sealed …

'It's about disdain.' ~ *Mobster reviews* Hamlet

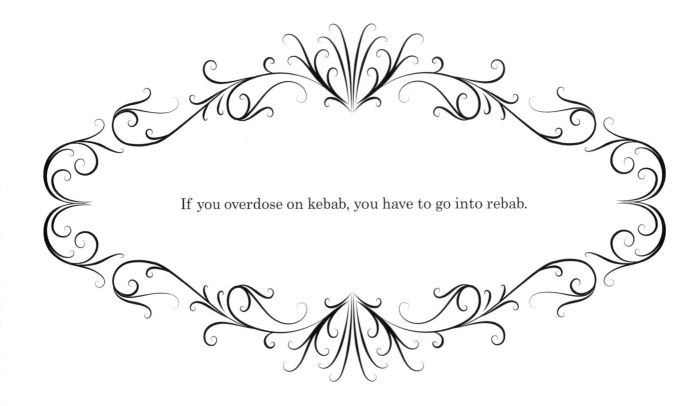

If you overdose on kebab, you have to go into rebab.

I like to put my Shredded Wheat

through my own shredder,

just to be on the safe side.

Ron Jeremy's first pet was called Jeremy,

and he grew up on Ron Street.

If you're ever in a hurry to get to the donkey sanctuary, just tell the driver 'donctuary'.

He'll know what you mean.

I imagine Superman must have some kind of reinforced toilet.

Woman: Thank you for not treating me as a doormat.

Man: You're welcome.

'Red eye at night,

you've been in a fight.'

I'll miss the Eiffel Tower when it launches.

There's a town called Only in America.

Only in America!

If you look at a woman's vagina under a microscope,

you can really spoil the evening.

When an elephant gets elephantitis, the doctor is like,

'Don't worry, that's normal.'

Italics give me a stiff neck.

Again, the publishers have rejected my novvle.

I just heard God sneeze,

but I don't know what to say to Him.

I never admit to feeling fear, I'm afraid.

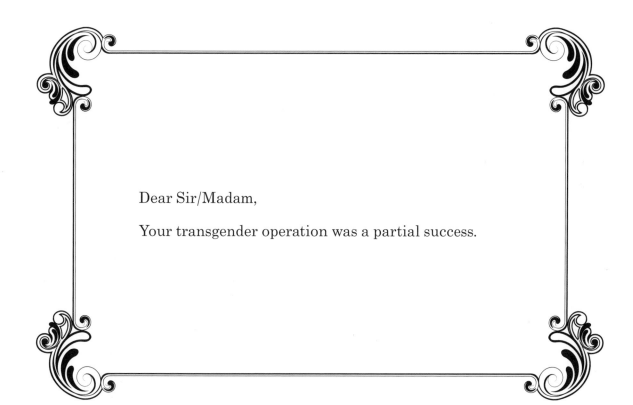

Dear Sir/Madam,

Your transgender operation was a partial success.

I like to think outside of the box, especially on a hot day.

You think asbestos is bad;

at least we don't still have asworstos.

I've lost my pet mosquito in amongst some normal ones.

Let's petition NASA to crack the Moon open.

I've got a feeling there's some pretty great stuff in there.

Slazenger *(n)*:

One who slazenges.

'Float like an octopus, sting like a clock.' ~ *Muhammad Dali*

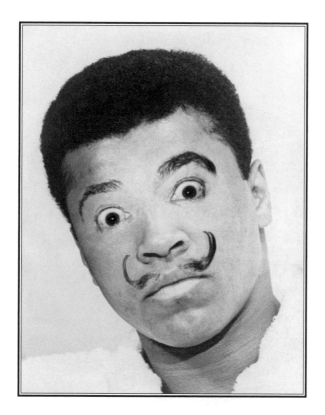

I love the Moon.

I'm so over it.

'Why would I need earwax?

I've got earwax coming out of my ears!'

I'm opening a burger chain for senior citizens

called Old McDonald's.

Reminiscing about my US coin collection.

Good dimes.

'Sometimes, a cigar is just a big dick. I mean cigar!!' ~

Sigmund Freud

The Earth used to be flat,

until God had the idea to inflate it.

The most complicated IKEA item to assemble

is the 'IKEA Store'.

If a man chooses to sleep with a
homeless guy every now and then,
that doesn't make him a hobosexual.

Women are like fine wines.

They're fine, but they whine.

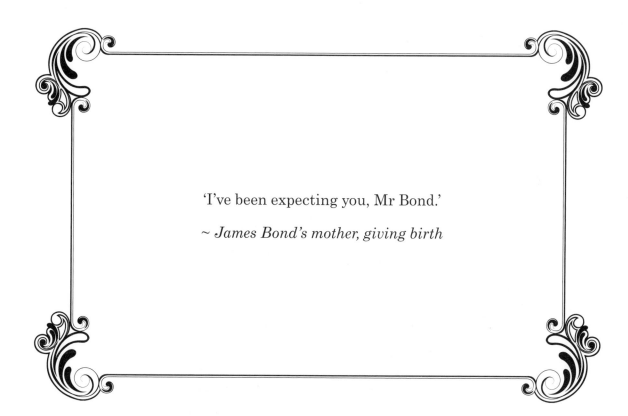

'I've been expecting you, Mr Bond.'

~ *James Bond's mother, giving birth*

I found a cow that produces chocolate milk!

It's pretty lumpy though, and man it stinks.

All films should end with the main actor waking up in bed saying,

'I just had the WEIRDEST dream.'

Man: Am I a gambling addict?

Doctor: You bet.

I like to keep in touch with my inner child

by swallowing little notes.

'I ... like to be quoted out of context.'

Scooby Doo episodes make perfect sense

if you imagine them

as Shaggy's hallucinations.

Shopkeeper: 'Debit or credit?'

Frog: 'Ribbit.'

Men often experience loss of internet due to bad wife-eye.

I've written a kids' version of *Snakes On A Plane*.

It's called *The Eels On The Bus*.

My sweet-smelling partner

Hates when I fartner.

I hope numbers never disappear.

Think of the aftermath.

Neuf, huit, sept, six,

I declare

Thumb peace.

I've got a lazy eye. It's on the sofa, as usual.

Those people in Eighties pornos were bonkers.

'What you did today was jaw-dropping. You're fired.' ~

Boss Paleontologist

I don't like to blow my own trumpet,

but I'm great at

blowing other people's trumpets.

The easiest way to win someone's heart

is to enter the hospital lottery.

A Golden Anniversary occurs when a couple have spent fifty years urinating on each other.

Boxers should never have sex during a fight.

'What do we want?'

'Now!'

'When do we want it?'

'Organisation!'

Lif is too short.

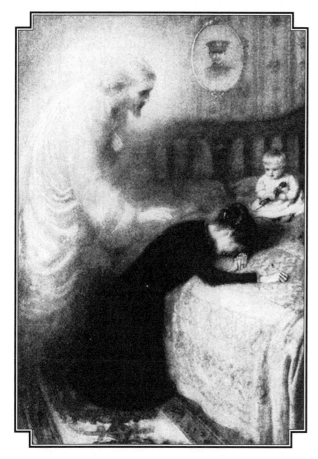

They called him 'Jesus Christ'

because he kept freaking people out.

Tried some of those new

refrigerated laxatives today.

Pretty cool shit.

'What am I, chopped liver?' ~

Chopped Liver

Imagine if birds  Dropped human-scale turds.

'She went Hathaway.' ~ *William Shakespeare*

Sometimes I just like to switch off.

I think that's why I lost my job in Intensive Care.

New *Viagra Soft*. For when she just wants to snuggle.™

I bumped into two people from Mercury today.

Small world.

DINNER PARTY ERROR:

The host could not be found.

Also, there was no response from the server.

I'm getting a tattoo that says 'One Day I Will Regret This.'

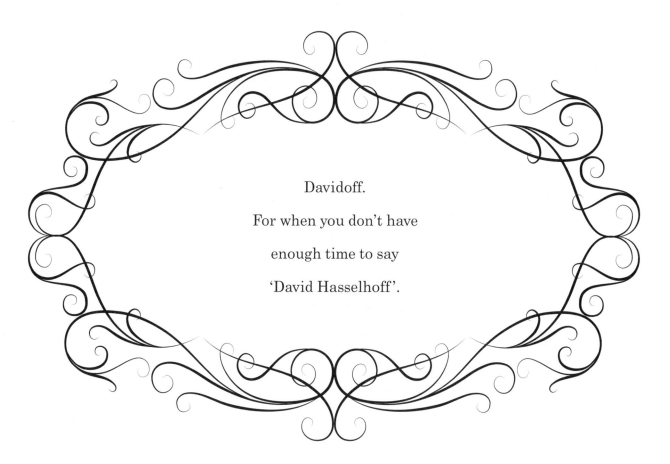

Davidoff.

For when you don't have

enough time to say

'David Hasselhoff'.

I have some skeletons in my closet.

I put my clothes on them.

Which end of a pregnancy tester are you supposed to poo on?

If you're reading a boring book,

turn all the full stops into

exclamation marks.

I wasn't laughing AT you, I was LAUGHING at you.

Soul singer CeCe Peniston still gets royalties whenever someone adds an extra email recipient.

I think people who support the death penalty

should be killed.

If someone says 'No thanks'

I like to reply, 'You're unwelcome'.

Centaur *(n)*: A creature with the body and legs of a horse, and the head, arms, torso and penis of a man.

There would be a weird atmosphere if

Peter Parker and Clark Kent

worked at the same newspaper.

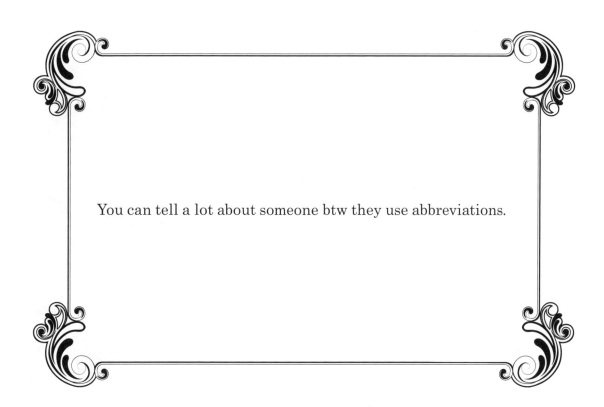

You can tell a lot about someone btw they use abbreviations.

Someone once accused me of grabbing their buttock.

The cheek!

Been reading about King Arthur.

What a legend.

Toilet warning: Never press the button marked 'reverse flush'.

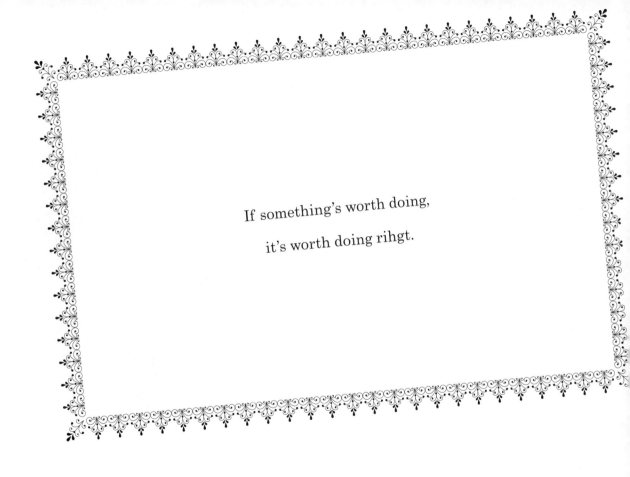

If something's worth doing,

it's worth doing rihgt.

The pen is mightier than the sword,

if it's a super 'Battle-Pen'.

I used to be scared of change.

Then I moved out of the wishing-well.

Noel's House Party still continues to this day,

although it is no longer televised.

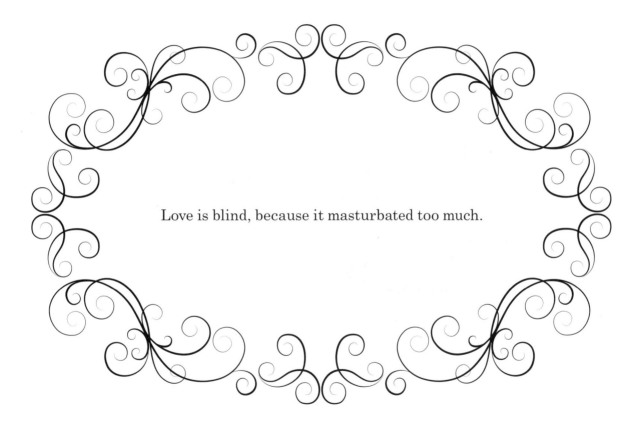

Love is blind, because it masturbated too much.

Tic-Tac-Toe *(n)*:

A form of gout caused by eating

too many mints.

If I could turn back time, I'd prevent Cher from recording that song.

Kids these days have Halloween too easy.

In my day, we had to make a lot of sacrifices.

I finally got round to reading

that Stephen Hawking book.

It's about time.

The longest-running TV series for ants is a cop show called

Insecticide.

Popeye's face looked like that

because he was allergic to spinach.

My dog has no-no's.

How does he smell?

He doesn't. That's one of his no-no's.

I bought the audiobook of *Where's Wally?'*

I still haven't heard him.

I hate it when people use the word 'shitstorm'.

Especially weathermen.

'That's another small step for man;

another giant leap for mankind.'

~ *Buzz Aldrin*, 1969

'Say hello to my little friend: Tiny Montana.'

If you make her frown,

turn her upside-down.

Dear Sir,

I forget to inform you that … um …

Is it wrong that I find women sexier if they've shaved their breasts?

Magneto's nemesis is Dr Fridge.

I wonder if Catherine Beta Jones still exists.

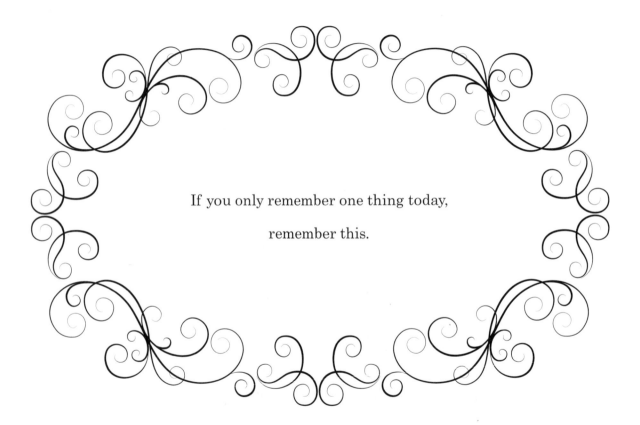

If you only remember one thing today,

remember this.

Tormented, tortured souls,

screaming in agony,

burning for eternity

in everlasting flames.

That'd be my idea of hell.

Most babies look like Winston Churchill

because he had sex with a lot of women.

Remember the Nineties,

when you had to clean your mouse balls?

I'm glad I don't have pets any more.

My ideal mermaid would have
the body of a woman and the
brain of a fish.

Bonsai trees are much larger these days.

And they seem to be everywhere.

If you ever fancy some Parma ham, but don't have any in the fridge,

just peel a bit of skin off your foot.

There are two kinds of people in the world,

and those who can't.

I rarely mix business with pleasure.

But when I do, I call it bupleasinuress.

The word 'replica' is a replica of the word 'replica'.

Revenge is a dish best smashed over someone's head.

Anxious lawyer suddenly thinks:

'I hope there are no more exhibits

after Exhibit Z.'

Internet pornography. What is the world coming to?

The animals in *The Flintstones* would have a much easier time now, with all the advances we've made in consumer technology.

'Baby, you're much more than my fuck-buddy.

You're my fuck-soulmate.'

Make sure your camel is genuine,

and not a llama with hump implants.

Iron Man also designs casual wear,

but that's not his strong suit.

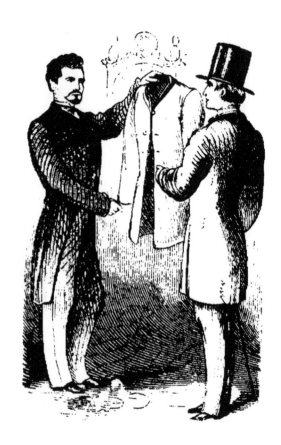

First thing I learned in Detective School:

every man has a pair of unique 'ballprints'.

Yesterday was the first day in the

reverse rest of your life.

Meat Loaf keeps trying to lose weight, but he's so delicious.

'If your penis be illin', take penicillin.' ~ *Alexander Fleming*

Do you sometimes get the strange feeling that you've never had déjà vu?

I love the Earth. It means the world to me.

I never learned to blink.

I have to sync my winks.

I'd love to purchase some Spice Girls forgetobilia.

Baby corn comes from Momcorn and Popcorn.

I'm afraid to let my mind wander, in case it never comes back.

'I avoided the Great Fire of London like the plague.' ~ *Samuel Pepys*

Dance music can be traced back to medieval times

when a farmer dropped some heavy beets.

All this time I thought I'd been lying to myself,

but I was just kidding myself.

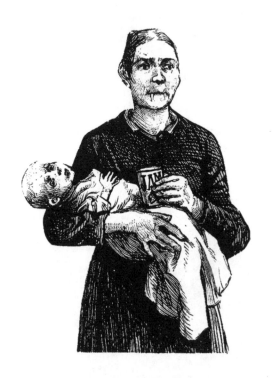

Vampire mothers usually start their babies on jam.

There are two parties in my pants! Well, 'balls'.

No matter how kinky you are,

sometimes you just fancy a onesome.

Reasons I'm never buying chicken drumsticks again.

1: Too short

2: Poor sound

3: Greasy snares, cymbals etc.

I've been diagnosed with very mild Tourette's, you nincompoop.

In Italy, certain ravioli can be used as postage stamps.

These days police can identify serial killers

simply by locating their serial number.

Sumo arm wrestlers just have one really fat arm.

A good treat for older kids is a Kinder Shock.

The Michelin Man looks jolly enough,

but I bet he doesn't clean between his 'folds' properly.

Gardeners make prize-winning cucumbers

by showing them pornography.

The thing I hate most about Christmas gifts

is the whole 'asking for reimbursement' part.

There's no 'I' in 'DENIAL'.

If you're out of avocados,

a good way to make guacamole is to blend The Incredible Hulk.

If corpses were alive, they'd be turning in their graves.

Jeremy Clarkson is like Marmite. Revolting.

Just found the Caps Lock button

on my head, for windy weather.

Quasimodo's hump was

actually a spare bell.

Abbreviation *(n)*:

Short for antibrevitudinalisation.

Goat prison inspector:

'Quite a ramshackle operation you have here.

Well done.'

I hate people who use the colloquial term to describe bodily spasms.

Jerks.

When a baby is born, I think the doctor should sing Happy Birthday.

'Some very sweaty geniuses are

actually 100% perspiration.'

~ Thomas Edison

Animal-doping jockeys should get off their high horses.

I hate the word 'thou'. It's so 'holier-than-you'.

Spider-Man's pyjamas are just a

looser-fitting version of his daytime suit.

Disgusted with my dictionary.

I found the term 'offensive'.

I'm seriously considering penis surgery,

if I can figure out how to hold a scalpel with it.

Most flight delays are caused by the plane suffering from jetlag.

Sheds are so-called because they were originally used to store old skin.

I never use those 24hr ATMs.

I need my cash now.

I mended the hole in my sock.

Now I can't get my foot in.

When I hear a news story begin 'It has emerged',

I wish the sentence would just end there.

Someday, I'd like to hear the patter of tiny feet.

Then later on, who knows?

We could try for a whole baby.

Ladies love Dracula,

until he reveals his tiny bat's penis.

I would hate myself if I became a narcissist.

The first robots were used by kings,

to put their robes on.

These Glade Plug-Ins haven't made

a bit of difference to the smell.

They're painful too.

Sky, why so blue?

Cheer up, it's a beautiful day!

Sewers. The toilets' toilets.

Sleep is something I can only dream about.

When you die, you unlock the
chance to play your life on
'Medium'.

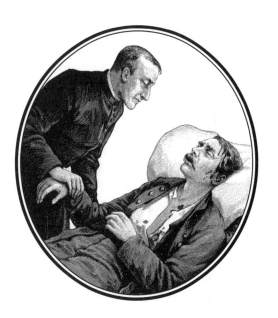

Every day, forest whales eat

millions of tons of planks.

I like to think of goths as pre-op vampires.

Just once, I'd like things to go from worse to bad.

I would describe myself as an animal lover, or 'carnivore'.

In maggot cinema, crowd scenes are

usually achieved with rice.

Snowmen have 600 words for 'Eskimo'.

I love hate. I have a love hate relationship.

We have nothing to fear except

fear of 'Itself'.

Did you know the dot below a question mark

is actually its dropping?

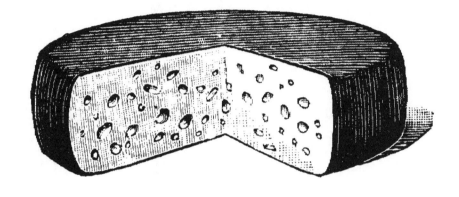

At a fancy restaurant, never ask for Swiss cheese.

Call it 'sparkling' cheese.

Trees are actually carved from

huge blocks of wood.

Pancake Recipe:

1. Melt pan.

When Edison had the idea to invent
the light bulb, he just used the one
that appeared above his head.

No two snowflakes like each other.

I don't think we can win the war on drugs.

We'd be too fucked-up to aim properly, etc.

My teachers said I was like a human sponge:

I'd sit in class, silently absorbing information,

then later, water would dribble out of me.

I've written a prequel to *Transformers*.

It's called *Sofabeds*.

As you'd expect, city minotaurs enjoy sleeping with women,

but country minotaurs prefer sex with cows.

Saliva is so delicious! Just thinking about it makes me drool.

The correct term for a worm's penis is its 'body'.

Punk scientist Ernest Rutherford was the first to spit on the atom.

Of all of Superman's achievements,

I think the best one is the Supermarket.

There's no business like business.

'Black sky at noon,

You're on the Moon.'

I can't wait until I become nostalgic for now.

Ahh, those will be the days.

If you ever run out of mercury for your thermometer,

just use a bit of robot sperm.

'Waiter, there's a fly in my soup. Thank you.'

Spider Restaurant

One-word review of *What's Eating Gilbert Grape*:

Leotard

Bathroom advice:

If your shower-head has different settings,

never choose the one labelled 'Mince'.

I regret buying that corrugated iron.

It's making my shirts MORE creased.

Historians studying the Pyramids still don't know

what scheme the Egyptians used

to pay for them.

I love all the different words Americans use for things,

but 'frosting' is the icing on the cake.

Trying to come up with a

concept for an internal hat.

I can't get my head around it.

Charles Dickens'
theory of evolution:
'Oliver Twist evolved
from a sea urchin.'

If toilets could talk, I'd probably

want to turn that function off.

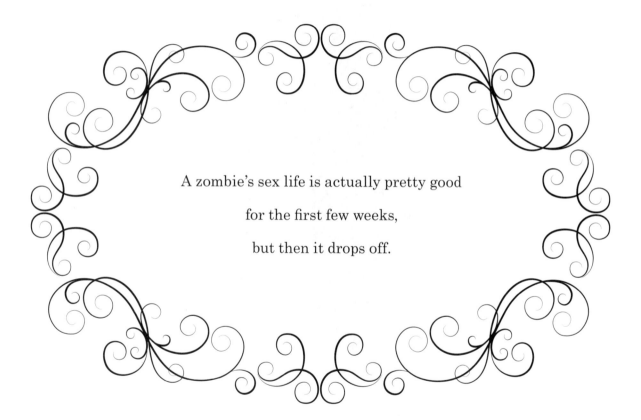

A zombie's sex life is actually pretty good

for the first few weeks,

but then it drops off.

'I'd like to return these convex contact lenses.'

If I forget what I'm supposed to be doing tomorrow,

I just call one of those psychic lines.

I hate the term 'MILF'. It's so crude.

I much prefer

'Female I'd Like to Take Home'.

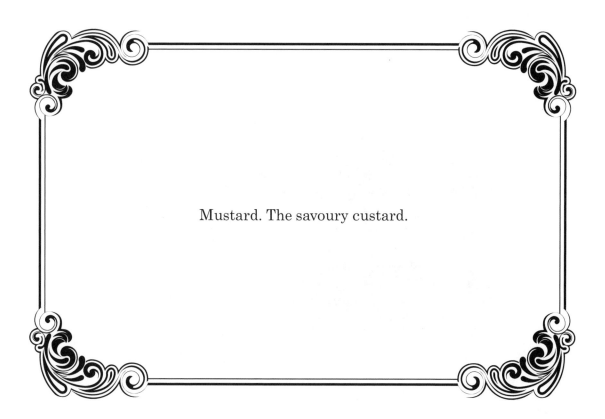

Mustard. The savoury custard.

If you see someone dancing, how do you know that

they're not just *pretending* to dance?

Laughter is the second best medicine.

The best medicine is medicine.

Pairs of shoes should come with a spare

'left/right combo shoe.'

Best cowboy phrase? 'Stick your hands up!'

Hands down.

Reasons the Sun landings were faked:

1. Too hot.

Some silent movies were so evocative,

you could almost hear piano music in your head.

I hate clichés in any way, shape or form.

The Eleventh Commandment:

Thou shall not use the word 'shalt'

'Six feet of soil?

Over my dead body.'

Babies haven't invented anything much

since the wah-wah pedal.

I was so tired last night,

all the people in my dreams were asleep.

I used to find buying books from Amazon slow and inconvenient,

until one day the receptionist suggested I use their website.

When Sigmund's glasses broke,

his wife took pleasure in seeing a shard in Freud.

I think my house is haunted by the ghost of an amoeba,

so it's not actually bothering me that much.

Trek Trivia: According to scientists, the original 1960's *Star Trek* theme is the music you hear when you commit suicide.

I've got a natural 'thing' with words.

Shame we can't see ultra-violet,

I bet it's beautiful.

Not so bothered about infra-red.

I wish my teeth were mint-flavoured – I'd save a fortune!

Also I wish my penis was sausage-flavoured.

Call me old-fashioned,

but I don't like these 'new' fashions.

Paris is probably the world's most romantic city,

at least until they finish MegaParis.

Cleanliness is next to godliness, in my non-alphabetical dictionary.

I love the smell of perfume.

If you could bottle it, you'd make a fortune.

The guy who named jazz music 'jazz' did a great job.

It's certainly the 'jazziest' type of music.

WARNING: This sentence contains

language which may fucking offend.

I wonder if I could achieve the perfect erection.

How hard could it be?

God has a plan for you. It's called 'death'.

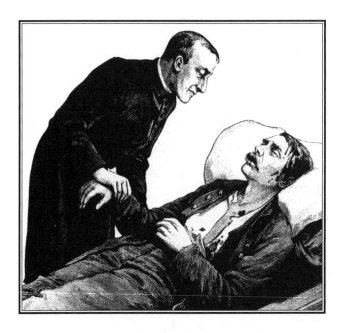

I care what people say,

I don't care what anybody says.

My diction is an utter shambles.

I can't utter 'shambles'.

'Well, that's two hours I will get back.' ~

Buddhist after watching terrible film

Here's something you never see.

The downside to being stinking rich

is the stinking.

Hey, Rainbow. Why'd you look so sad?

Farts are how bottoms

communicate with each other.

It's not the winning, it's the taking part that's unimportant.

I'd like to join a golf club

to another golf club.

The eyes are the windows to the soul, especially if they're glass eyes.

It must be awful if you're an architect

and you get apartment block.

You snooze, you lose. But at least you've had a snooze.

Masturbation is only cheating if you do it behind your own back.

It never rains, but it pours. Except when it just rains.

Love never dies.

It just gets old.

How philosophers greet each other:

'Hello, why are you?'

Having sex without taking your clothes off is

the most fun you can have without taking your clothes off.

How dare you call me a bad Christian.

I know the Lord's Prayer backwards!

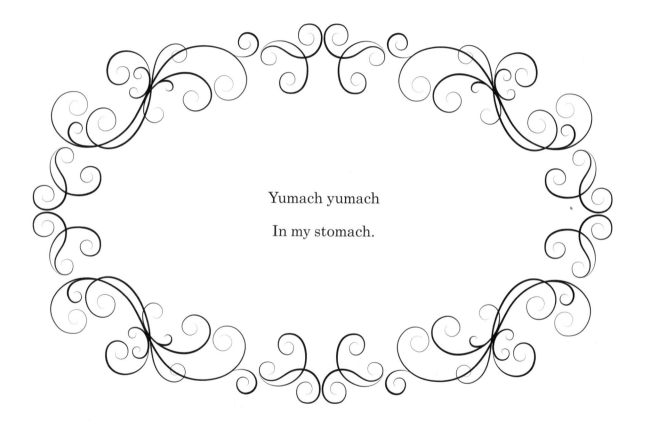

Yumach yumach

In my stomach.

I'm making a device that listens to people's minds.

I'd love to hear your thoughts.

The Elephant Man also had

a massive you-know-what,

so you know, every cloud.

I'd like to change my name to Deed Poll.

Need a big golf ball? Just chew on a cueball.

Plants take pictures of keyboards using photosynthesis.

I feel sorry for people with just one nostril,

who can only smell in mono.

'Oh yeah, I REALLY hate cigars.' ~ *Fidel Sarcastro*

If you want to cheerfully disagree with someone,

just say 'Nokey dokey!'

I like to think of straight women

as gay lesbians.

Nervert *(n)*: A nervous pervert.

I'd hate it if someone discovered my sex tape,

or as I call it, 'duct tape.'

They never mention it, but Doctor Who's speciality is

genito-urinary infections.

I wish my postman wouldn't deliver my voicemail.

His accent is awful.

'What's the antimatter?'

'Oh, nothing.'

I wonder when they'll open Jurassic Park again.

Contact lenses make excellent baby monocles.

I'm so literal, I'd be late for my own funeral.

Jim Henson's first job

was operating the *Godfather* logo.

Farmer: I'd like to give my sheep a sex-change.

Vet: Are you aware of the ramifications?

Constipation makes me so angry, I could shit.

I like to undress women with my eyes.

It takes a lot longer.

I have noblem shortening words.

Real reason why the dinosaurs are extinct:

The museum industry.

Labiarinth *(n)*:

An extremely complicated vagina.

Whenever Chewbacca loses his voice, he talks by dragging

heavy furniture across the floor.

When is *Inception* going to finish?

A good way to treat a sex addict is to take him for a nice sexy day out.

Remember when everyone used to say 'Join the club'?

Join the club.

I went back in time and killed Über-Hitler.

That's why you've never heard of him.

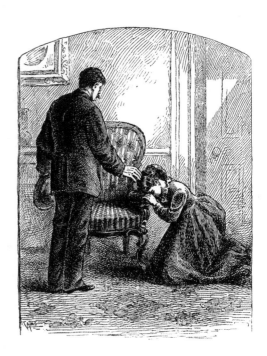

Nothing rhymes with nothing.

The final version of James Brown's *Sex Machine*

contained over 14,000 moving parts.

Usually I have a hard-off.

I think pigs have that curious smile because

they know how delicious they are.

Unexpect the unexpected.

If you ever need a cactus in a hurry,

just make a cucumber angry.

My false alarm has gone off, and I don't know what to do.

When I heard the news that the Notorious BIG had died, it didn't really affect me.

No Biggie.

I really need to improve my 'word-list'.

Toilets invented toilet paper to use for their writings,

but humans were not impressed.

I know I'm losing it when

I start talking to myselves.

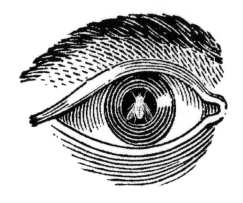

I'd love to be a fly on the wall of the *Big Brother* house.

Henry VIII predicted reggae music, but could never prove it.

How would I know? I'm not a mindreader.

I'm such a 'people snob'.

I wonder how zombies tell the difference between

normal and 'special-needs' zombies.

If I see a picture of the sun wearing sunglasses,

that can sidetrack me for hours.

I'm hosting my first orgy tonight.

I hope people come.

'This is what it sounds like when doves cry.'

~ Prince, listening to pigeons cry

I wonder if ants behaved any differently during Medieval times, or were they pretty much the same as now?

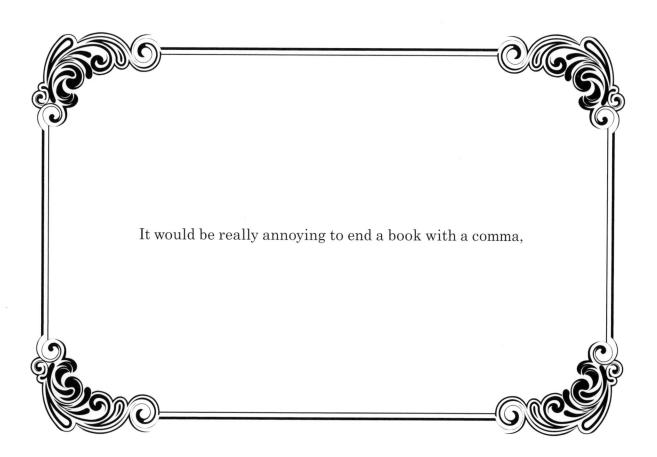

It would be really annoying to end a book with a comma,

Thanks to:

My parents Cathy and Abe, my children, Sam and Phoebe, for their endless inspiration, my brother James and sister Helen, Granddad Jim for kindly allowing me to use his picture on page 10, Robert Popper (hetto!), David Walliams for suggesting the title, Jimmy Carr for his generous help and encouragement, Susan and Timothy Langdale, Graham Linehan, Xeni Jardin, Maria Schneider, my agent Jonny Geller, Lisa Babalis, Conor McCaughan at Troika, Josh Katz at UTA, Jon Butler at Macmillan, Patrick Ewing at Twitter, Lee Thomas, John Hodgman, Luz Diaz, Liam Lynch, Will Arnett, Mitch Hurwitz, Jim Vallely, Justin Theroux, Rob Delaney and Megan Amram.

A huge thank you to my incredible designer Alex Morris (*pinvin.com*), whose patience, skill and comic brain enhanced the words so much.

A special thanks to the immensely talented James Hance (*jameshance.com*) for the painting used on the back cover, and some of the preliminary illustrations (especially Tiny Montana).

Thank you to all who follow me on Twitter.

And thanks finally to Satan, without whose guiding hand and undying hate this book would not have happened.